THE ART OF WAR
VISUALIZED
THE SUN TZU CLASSIC IN CHARTS AND GRAPHS

THE ART OF WAR

VISUALIZED

THE SUN TZU CLASSIC IN CHARTS AND GRAPHS

JESSICA HAGY

WORKMAN PUBLISHING, NEW YORK

The English translation of the text of *The Art of War* was made by Lionel Giles and was first published in 1910 by Luzac & Co., London.

Library of Congress Cataloging-in-Publication Data is available.
ISBNs: 978-0-7611-8238-2 (pb); 978-0-7611-8493-5 (hc)

Design by Sarah Smith

Workman books are available at special discounts when purchased in bulk for premiums and sales promotions as well as for fund-raising or educational use. Special editions or book excerpts also can be created to specification. For details, contact the Special Sales Director at the address below, or send an email to specialmarkets@workman.com.

Workman Publishing Company, Inc.
225 Varick Street
New York, NY 10014-4381

workman.com

Workman is a registered trademark of Workman Publishing Co., Inc.

Printed in the United States of America
First printing February 2015
10 9 8 7 6 5 4 3 2 1

FOR CALVIN

Here's to fighting thoughtfully for only the best of causes.

CONTENTS

INTRODUCTION

VISUALIZE YOUR METAPHOR

The *Art of War* is a classic text attributed to the Chinese general Sun Tzu, who lived roughly 2,500 years ago. In recent centuries, it's become not only *the* must-read book on military strategy (obviously), but it's also become the go-to guide for domination in business, politics, management, marketing, logistical planning, and even sports. It has a concise, biblical rhythm, and a vaguely mythical tone. It's so old and so mysterious that it is *literally* legendary.

Because I'm a visual storyteller by trade, when I first read *The Art of War*, I saw the short verses as captions for images that weren't yet on the page; reimagining this globally revered classic with charts and graphs was something I felt almost compelled to do—to create a modern, visual translation that shakes off 2,500 years of dust and changes the way we ponder conflict. At first, illustrating it was a challenge. But halfway through the second chapter, I realized that his ideas aren't as bloodthirsty and brutish as his legend might lead you to believe. I found I actually liked old Sun Tzu. He makes a lot (and I do mean a *lot*) of logical sense. Each of his verses is a kind of lesson, so feel free to hopscotch through the pages or pause to reflect as you go along—after all, the most important verses in this book will be the ones that help you best visualize your own experiences.

It became clear that *The Art of War* is massively popular because Sun Tzu's insights apply to all conflicts, great or small. The advice in these pages is as applicable to a ten-year-old running for student council president as it is to a conquering general. It's less about war than it is about problem solving—it's a meta-metaphor. War is merely the stand-in noun for every hassle you've ever had in your life. We're all fighting for something or other. Lucky for us, Sun Tzu gave us a game plan.

PROTAGONIST
VS.
SELF

PROTAGONIST
VS.
OTHERS

PROTAGONIST
VS.
NATURE

Sun Tzu tackles them all, and so do all of us.

CHAPTER 1
LAYING
PLANS

VISUALIZE YOUR STRATEGY

Sun Tzu said:

The art of war* is of vital importance to the State.

It is a matter of life and death, a road either to safety or to ruin.

Hence it is a subject of inquiry which can on no account be neglected.

SURVIVAL

*

STRATEGY

The art of war, then, is governed by five constant factors, to be taken into account in one's deliberations, when seeking to determine the conditions obtaining in the field.

These are:

1. The Moral Law
2. Heaven
3. Earth
4. The Commander
5. Method and discipline

event planning

LOGISTICS

LEADERSHIP

PROFESSIONALISM

MARKET FORCES

ETHICS

The Moral Law causes the people to be in complete accord with their ruler, so that they will follow him regardless of their lives, undismayed by any danger.

Heaven signifies night and day, cold and heat, times and seasons. Earth comprises distances, great and small; danger and security; open ground and narrow passes; the chances of life and death.

The Commander stands for the virtues of wisdom, sincerity, benevolence, courage, and strictness.

By method and discipline are to be understood the marshaling of the army in its proper subdivisions, the graduations of rank among the officers, the maintenance of roads by which supplies may reach the army, and the control of military expenditure.

METHOD

DISCIPLINE

professionals

feral children

These five heads should be familiar to every general:

He who knows them will be victorious; he who knows them not will fail.

Therefore, in your deliberations, when seeking to determine the military conditions, let them be made the basis of a comparison, in this wise:

before you make a move

COMPARE

CALCULATE

CONTRAST

Which of the two sovereigns is imbued with the Moral Law?

Which of the two generals has most ability? With whom lie the advantages derived from Heaven and Earth?

On which side is discipline most rigorously enforced? Which army is stronger? On which side are officers and men more highly trained?

In which army is there the greater constancy both in reward and punishment?

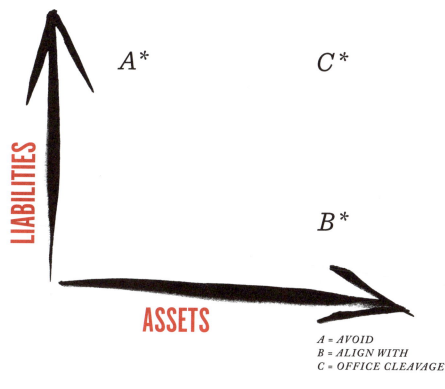

A*

C*

LIABILITIES

B*

ASSETS

A = AVOID
B = ALIGN WITH
C = OFFICE CLEAVAGE

By means of these seven considerations I can forecast victory or defeat.

The general who hearkens to my counsel and acts upon it, will conquer: Let such a one be retained in command!

The general who hearkens not to my counsel nor acts upon it, will suffer defeat: Let such a one be dismissed!

LISTEN CLOSELY

keep your job

ACT ON WHAT YOU HEAR

While heeding the profit of my counsel, avail yourself also of any helpful circumstances over and beyond the ordinary rules.

According as circumstances are favorable, one should modify one's plans.

All warfare is based on deception.

Hence, when able to attack, we must seem unable; when using our forces, we must seem inactive; when we are near, we must make the enemy believe we are far away; when far away, we must make him believe we are near,

honest

forthright

transparent

EASILY CONQUERED & VERY HARD TO FIND

Hold out baits to entice the enemy.

Feign disorder, and crush him.

If he is secure at all points, be prepared for him. If he is in superior strength, evade him.

If your opponent is of choleric temper, seek to irritate him. Pretend to be weak, that he may grow arrogant.

If he is taking his ease, give him no rest. If his forces are united, separate them.

Attack him where he is unprepared, appear where you are not expected.

These military devices, leading to victory, must not be divulged beforehand.

VULNERABILITY

WEAKNESS

opportunity

Now the general who wins a battle makes many calculations in his temple ere the battle is fought.

The general who loses a battle makes but few calculations beforehand.

Thus do many calculations lead to victory, and few calculations to defeat: how much more no calculation at all!

It is by attention to this point that I can foresee who is likely to win or lose.

LAUGHABLE

Crystal ball on the table

PREDICTING THE FUTURE

Experience in the field

BELIEVABLE

CHAPTER 2
WAGING WAR

VISUALIZE YOUR APPROACH

Sun Tzu said:

In the operations of war, where there are in the field a thousand swift chariots, as many heavy chariots, and a hundred thousand mail-clad soldiers, with provisions enough to carry them a thousand *li*, the expenditure at home and at the front, including entertainment of guests, small items such as glue and paint, and sums spent on chariots and armor, will reach the total of a thousand ounces of silver per day.

Such is the cost of raising an army of 100,000 men.

A = college   B = condoms

When you engage in actual fighting, if victory is long in coming, then men's weapons will grow dull and their ardor will be damped.

If you lay siege to a town, you will exhaust your strength.

Again, if the campaign is protracted, the resources of the State will not be equal to the strain.

Now, when your weapons are dulled, your ardor damped, your strength exhausted, and your treasure spent, other chieftains will spring up to take advantage of your extremity.

Then no man, however wise, will be able to avert the consequences that must ensue.

Thus, though we have heard of stupid haste in war, cleverness has never been seen associated with long delays.

A FIGHTING CHANCE

ACTION

THOUGHT

There is no instance of a country having benefited from prolonged warfare.

It is only one who is thoroughly acquainted with the evils of war who can thoroughly understand the profitable way of carrying it on.

> The skillful soldier does not raise a second levy, neither are his supply-wagons loaded more than twice.
>
> Bring war material with you from home, but forage on the enemy.
>
> Thus the army will have food enough for its needs.

therapy

resourcefulness

PROBLEMS

BAGGAGE

Poverty of the State exchequer causes an army to be maintained by contributions from a distance. Contributing to maintain an army at a distance causes the people to be impoverished.

On the other hand, the proximity of an army causes prices to go up; and high prices cause the people's substance to be drained away.

When their substance is drained away, the peasantry will be afflicted by heavy exactions.

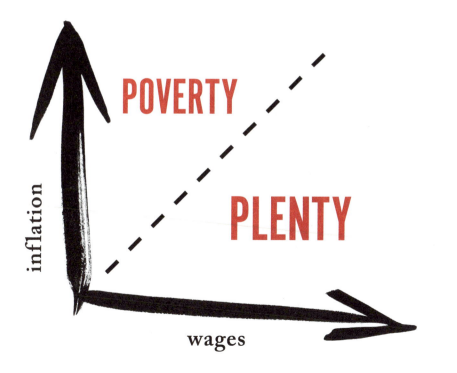

With this loss of substance and exhaustion of strength, the homes of the people will be stripped bare, and three-tenths of their income will be dissipated; while government expenses for broken chariots, worn-out horses, breast-plates and helmets, bows and arrows, spears and shields, protective mantles, draught-oxen, and heavy wagons will amount to four-tenths of its total revenue.

MONEY SENT FROM HOME

how dynasties crumble

POOR FUTURE PROSPECTS

Hence a wise general makes a point of foraging on the enemy.

One cartload of the enemy's provisions is equivalent to twenty of one's own, and likewise a single *picul* of his provender is equivalent to twenty from one's own store.

HUSTLE

ASSETS

carpe *EVERYTHING*

Now in order to kill the enemy, our men must be roused to anger; that there may be advantage from defeating the enemy, they must have their rewards.

Therefore in chariot fighting, when ten or more chariots have been taken, those should be rewarded who took the first.

Our own flags should be substituted for those of the enemy*, and the chariots mingled and used in conjunction with ours.

The captured soldiers should be kindly treated and kept.

This is called using the conquered foe to augment one's own strength.

ASSIMILATION

UNITE = CONQUER

In war, then, let your great object be victory, not lengthy campaigns.

Thus it may be known that the leader of armies is the arbiter of the people's fate, the man on whom it depends whether the nation shall be in peace or in peril.

A = duration of war
B = cost to state
C = trust in leaders

CHAPTER 3

ATTACK BY STRATAGEM

VISUALIZE YOUR ANGLE

Sun Tzu said:

In the practical art of war, the best thing of all is to take the enemy's country whole and intact; to shatter and destroy it is not so good.

So, too, it is better to recapture an army entire than to destroy it, to capture a regiment, a detachment, or a company entire than to destroy them.

Hence to fight and conquer in all your battles is not supreme excellence; supreme excellence consists in breaking the enemy's resistance without fighting.

SPOILS

DESTRUCTION

Thus the highest form of generalship is to balk the enemy's plans; the next best is to prevent the junction of the enemy's forces; the next in order is to attack the enemy's army in the field; and the worst policy of all is to besiege walled cities.

The rule is, not to besiege walled cities if it can possibly be avoided.

The preparation of mantlets, movable shelters, and various implements of war will take up three whole months; and the piling up of mounds over against the walls will take three months more.

UNDERMINE OVERTAKE

bullying & sanctions

The general, unable to control his irritation, will launch his men to the assault like swarming ants, with the result that one-third of his men are slain, while the town still remains untaken.

Such are the disastrous effects of a siege.

ignore

freak out

WISDOM

FOOLISHNESS

ANNOYANCE

Therefore the skillful leader subdues the enemy's troops without any fighting; he captures their cities without laying siege to them; he overthrows their kingdom without lengthy operations in the field.

With his forces intact he will dispute the mastery of the Empire, and thus, without losing a man, his triumph will be complete.

This is the method of attacking by stratagem.

seduction

success

POSITIONING YOURSELF WELL

It is the rule in war, if our forces are ten to the enemy's one, to surround him; if five to one, to attack him; if twice as numerous, to divide our army into two.

If equally matched, we can offer battle; if slightly inferior in numbers, we can avoid the enemy; if quite unequal in every way, we can flee from him.

Hence, though an obstinate fight may be made by a small force, in the end it must be captured by the larger force.

YOU ARE STRONGER

YOU ARE BIGGER

the battle you should choose

YOU ARE SMARTER

Now the general is the bulwark of the State; if the bulwark is complete at all points, the State will be strong; if the bulwark is defective, the State will be weak.

GAIN SUPPORT

SHOW LEADERSHIP

There are three ways in which a ruler can bring misfortune upon his army:

1. By commanding the army to advance or to retreat, being ignorant of the fact that it cannot obey. This is called hobbling the army.

2. By attempting to govern an army in the same way as he administers a kingdom, being ignorant of the conditions which obtain in an army. This causes restlessness in the soldiers' minds.

3. By employing the officers of his army without discrimination, through ignorance of the military principle of adaptation to circumstances. This shakes the confidence of the soldiers.

IGNORANCE

ACTION

FAILURE

But when the army is restless and distrustful, trouble is sure to come from the other feudal princes.

This is simply bringing anarchy into the army, and flinging victory away.

DISMAY

LOYALTY FALTERS

ALTERNATIVES PRESENT THEMSELVES

Thus we may know that there are five essentials for victory:

1. He will win who knows when to fight and when not to fight.

2. He will win who knows how to handle both superior and inferior forces.

3. He will win whose army is animated by the same spirit throughout all its ranks.

4. He will win who, prepared himself, waits to take the enemy unprepared.

5. He will win who has military capacity and is not interfered with by the sovereign.

HOW GOOD WORK GETS DONE

GUIDES TO FOLLOW

BOSSES WHO GET OUT OF THE WAY

PEOPLE TO LEAD

Hence the saying: If you know the enemy and know yourself, you need not fear the result of a hundred battles.

If you know yourself but not the enemy, for every victory gained you will also suffer a defeat.

If you know neither the enemy nor yourself, you will succumb in every battle.

KNOW YOUR ENEMY

KNOW YOURSELF

The Art of War (in a nutshell)

CHAPTER 4

TACTICAL DISPOSITIONS

VISUALIZE YOUR ADVANTAGES

Sun Tzu said:

The good fighters of old first put themselves beyond the possibility of defeat, and then waited for an opportunity of defeating the enemy.

To secure ourselves against defeat lies in our own hands, but the opportunity of defeating the enemy is provided by the enemy himself.

FAILURE

viable options

OPPORTUNITIES

AWARENESS

Thus the good fighter is able to secure himself against defeat, but cannot make certain of defeating the enemy.

Hence the saying: One may know how to conquer without being able to do it.

intelligence

defense

1/2
THE BATTLE

Security against defeat implies defensive tactics; ability to defeat the enemy means taking the offensive.

Standing on the defensive indicates insufficient strength; attacking, a superabundance of strength.

CONFIDENCE

defensiveness

The general who is skilled in defense hides in the most secret recesses of the earth; he who is skilled in attack flashes forth from the topmost heights of heaven.

Thus on the one hand we have ability to protect ourselves; on the other, a victory that is complete.

HIDE

SEEK

small children **&** masters of surprise

To see victory only when it is within the ken of the common herd is not the acme of excellence.

Neither is it the acme of excellence if you fight and conquer and the whole Empire says, "Well done!"

COMMONPLACE

A WIN ONLY ON PAPER

SIMPLE

easy As

To lift an autumn hair is no sign of great strength; to see the sun and moon is no sign of sharp sight; to hear the noise of thunder is no sign of a quick ear.

What the ancients called a clever fighter is one who not only wins, but excels in winning with ease.

Hence his victories bring him neither reputation for wisdom nor credit for courage.

LOOKS EFFORTLESS

REQUIRES TRUE SKILL

modern art

He wins his battles by making no mistakes.

Making no mistakes is what establishes the certainty of victory, for it means conquering an enemy that is already defeated.

Hence the skillful fighter puts himself into a position which makes defeat impossible, and does not miss the moment for defeating the enemy.

losers

GOOFS

FLUBS

Thus it is that in war the victorious strategist only seeks battle after the victory has been won, whereas he who is destined to defeat first fights and afterwards looks for victory.

The consummate leader cultivates the Moral Law, and strictly adheres to method and discipline; thus it is in his power to control success.

IMPULSIVE

the opposite of leadership

EMOTIONAL

In respect of military method, we have, firstly, Measurement; secondly, Estimation of quantity; thirdly, Calculation; fourthly, Balancing of chances; fifthly, Victory.

Measurement owes its existence to Earth; Estimation of quantity to Measurement; Calculation to Estimation of quantity; Balancing of chances to Calculation; and Victory to Balancing of chances.

MEASURE

ESTIMATE

BALANCE

CALCULATE

A = before you act

A victorious army opposed to a routed one, is as a pound's weight placed in the scale against a single grain.

The onrush of a conquering force is like the bursting of pent-up waters into a chasm a thousand fathoms deep.

 = *measure often, attack once*

CHAPTER 5
ENERGY

VISUALIZE
YOUR
RESOURCES

Sun Tzu said:

The control of a large force is the same principle as the control of a few men: It is merely a question of dividing up their numbers.

Fighting with a large army under your command is nowise different from fighting with a small one: It is merely a question of instituting signs and signals.

COMMUNICATE

ALLOCATE

DELEGATE

how to lead large groups

To ensure that your whole host may withstand the brunt of the enemy's attack and remain unshaken—this is effected by maneuvers direct and indirect.

That the impact of your army may be like a grindstone dashed against an egg—this is effected by the science of weak points and strong.

In all fighting, the direct method may be used for joining battle, but indirect methods will be needed in order to secure victory.

Indirect tactics, efficiently applied, are inexhaustible as Heaven and Earth, unending as the flow of rivers and streams;

like the sun and moon, they end but to begin anew; like the four seasons, they pass away to return once more.

creativity

INEXHAUSTIBLE RESOURCES

COMPETITIVE ADVANTAGE

There are not more than five musical notes, yet the combinations of these five give rise to more melodies than can ever be heard.

There are not more than five primary colors (blue, yellow, red, white, and black), yet in combination they produce more hues than can ever been seen.

There are not more than five cardinal tastes (sour, acrid, salt, sweet, bitter), yet combinations of them yield more flavors than can ever be tasted.

COMBINATIONS

FUNDAMENTALS

every play in every book

In battle, there are not more than two methods of attack—
the direct and the indirect; yet these two in combination
give rise to an endless series of maneuvers.

The direct and the indirect lead on to each other in turn.

It is like moving in a circle—you never come to an end.

Who can exhaust the possibilities of their combination?

The onset of troops is like the rush of a torrent which will even roll stones along in its course.

The quality of decision is like the well-timed swoop of a falcon which enables it to strike and destroy its victim.

Therefore the good fighter will be terrible in his onset, and prompt in his decision.

Energy may be likened to the bending of a crossbow; decision, to the releasing of a trigger.

Amid the turmoil and tumult of battle, there may be seeming disorder and yet no real disorder at all; amid confusion and chaos, your array may be without head or tail, yet it will be proof against defeat.

Simulated disorder postulates perfect discipline; simulated fear postulates courage; simulated weakness postulates strength.

Hiding order beneath the cloak of disorder is simply a question of subdivision; concealing courage under a show of timidity presupposes a fund of latent energy; masking strength with weakness is to be effected by tactical dispositions.

Thus one who is skillful at keeping the enemy on the move maintains deceitful appearances, according to which the enemy will act. He sacrifices something, that the enemy may snatch at it.

By holding out baits, he keeps him on the march; then with a body of picked men he lies in wait for him.

DECEPTION = ADVANTAGE

The clever combatant looks to the effect of combined energy, and does not require too much from individuals.

Hence his ability to pick out the right men and utilize combined energy.

TEAMWORK

MORALE

CARROTS

STICKS

HAZING

When he utilizes combined energy, his fighting men become as it were like unto rolling logs or stones.

For it is the nature of a log or stone to remain motionless on level ground, and to move when on a slope; if four-cornered, to come to a standstill, but if round-shaped, to go rolling down.

Thus the energy developed by good fighting men is as the momentum of a round stone rolled down a mountain thousands of feet in height.

So much on the subject of energy.

*avalanches &
public relations*

CRUSHING POWER

MOMENTUM

CHAPTER 6

WEAK POINTS AND STRONG

VISUALIZE YOUR OPPORTUNITIES

Sun Tzu said:

Whoever is first in the field and awaits the coming of the enemy will be fresh for the fight; whoever is second in the field and has to hasten to battle will arrive exhausted.

Therefore the clever combatant imposes his will on the enemy, but does not allow the enemy's will to be imposed on him.

By holding out advantages to him, he can cause the enemy to approach of his own accord; or, by inflicting damage, he can make it impossible for the enemy to draw near.

TERRIFY

drive away

ANTAGONIZE

draw in

TEMPT

If the enemy is taking his ease, he can harass him; if well supplied with food, he can starve him out; if quietly encamped, he can force him to move.

Appear at points which the enemy must hasten to defend; march swiftly to places where you are not expected.

IDENTIFY SOURCES OF JOY

DESTROY THEM

how to kill a soul

An army may march great distances without distress, if it marches through country where the enemy is not.

You can be sure of succeeding in your attacks if you only attack places which are undefended.

You can ensure the safety of your defense if you only hold positions that cannot be attacked.

Hence that general is skillful in attack whose opponent does not know what to defend; and he is skillful in defense whose opponent does not know what to attack.

DEFENSES UP

NASTY PEOPLE NEARBY

why people drink after work

O divine art of subtlety and secrecy!

Through you we learn to be invisible, through you inaudible;
and hence we can hold the enemy's fate in our hands.

secret sauces

INSIGHTS

ADVANTAGES

You may advance and be absolutely irresistible if you make for the enemy's weak points; you may retire and be safe from pursuit if your movements are more rapid than those of the enemy.

staying ahead & alive

SWIFT MOVES

WEAK TARGETS

If we wish to fight, the enemy can be forced to an engagement even though he be sheltered behind a high rampart and a deep ditch.

All we need do is attack some other place that he will be obliged to relieve.

If we do not wish to fight, we can prevent the enemy from engaging us even though the lines of our encampment be merely traced out on the ground.

All we need do is to throw something odd and unaccountable in his way.

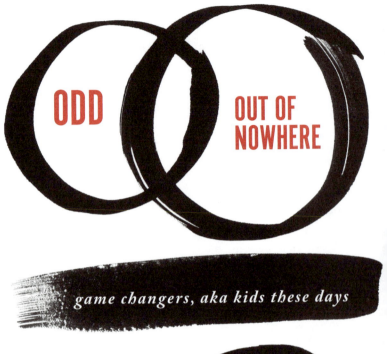

ODD

OUT OF NOWHERE

game changers, aka kids these days

INTRIGUING

DIFFERENT

By discovering the enemy's dispositions and remaining invisible ourselves, we can keep our forces concentrated, while the enemy's must be divided.

We can form a single united body, while the enemy must split up into fractions.

Hence there will be a whole pitted against separate parts of a whole, which means that we shall be many to the enemy's few.

STRENGTH

FULL SILOS

● *grain*

● *information*

And if we are able thus to attack an inferior force with a superior one, our opponents will be in dire straits.

GUNFIGHT

KNIFE

shoddy intelligence work

The spot where we intend to fight must not be made known; for then the enemy will have to prepare against a possible attack at several different points; and his forces being thus distributed in many directions, the numbers we shall have to face at any given point will be proportionately few.

imminent bankruptcy

For should the enemy strengthen his van, he will weaken his rear; should he strengthen his rear, he will weaken his van; should he strengthen his left, he will weaken his right; should he strengthen his right, he will weaken his left.

If he sends reinforcements everywhere, he will everywhere be weak.

Numerical weakness comes from having to prepare against possible attacks; numerical strength, from compelling our adversary to make these preparations against us.

Knowing the place and the time of the coming battle, we may concentrate from the greatest distances in order to fight.

how to win before you fight

SIMPLIFY

ORGANIZE

SCHEDULE

But if neither time nor place be known, then the left wing will be impotent to succor the right, the right equally impotent to succor the left, the van unable to relieve the rear, or the rear to support the van.

How much more so if the furthest portions of the army are anything under a hundred *li* apart, and even the nearest are separated by several *li*!

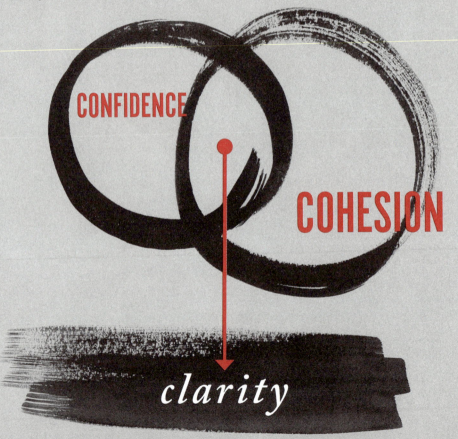

Though according to my estimate the soldiers of Yueh exceed our own in number, that shall advantage them nothing in the matter of victory.

I say then that victory can be achieved.

deadly poison & strategic underdogs

POWERFUL

EFFICIENT

SMALL

Though the enemy be stronger in numbers, we may prevent him from fighting.

Schemc so as to discover his plans and the likelihood of their success.

HOW EASY IT IS TO HURT THEM

HOW WELL YOU KNOW SOMEONE

Rouse him, and learn the principle of his activity or inactivity.

Force him to reveal himself, so as to find out his vulnerable spots.

Carefully compare the opposing army with your own, so that you may know where strength is superabundant and where it is deficient.

CONTRAST

COMPARE

CRITIQUE

prepare for debates & battles

In making tactical dispositions, the highest pitch you can attain is to conceal them; conceal your dispositions, and you will be safe from the prying of the subtlest spies, from the machinations of the wisest brains.

How victory may be produced for them out of the enemy's own tactics—that is what the multitude cannot comprehend.

INTENSE STUDY

STRATEGIZING

the heavy lifting done behind the scenes

All men can see the tactics whereby I conquer, but what none can see is the strategy out of which victory is evolved.

Do not repeat the tactics which have gained you one victory, but let your methods be regulated by the infinite variety of circumstances.

SURVIVAL

REINVENTION

Military tactics are like unto water; for water in its natural course runs away from high places and hastens downwards.

So in war, the way is to avoid what is strong and to strike at what is weak.

Water shapes its course according to the nature of the ground over which it flows; the soldier works out his victory in relation to the foe whom he is facing.

Therefore, just as water retains no constant shape, so in warfare there are no constant conditions.

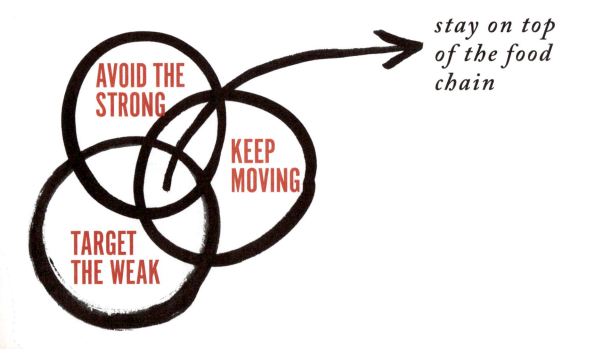

He who can modify his tactics in relation to his opponent and thereby succeed in winning, may be called a heaven-born captain.

The five elements (water, fire, wood, metal, earth) are not always equally predominant; the four seasons make way for each other in turn.

There are short days and long; the moon has its periods of waning and waxing.

SUCCESS

ADAPTABILITY

CHAPTER 7
MANEUVERING

VISUALIZE
YOUR
NARRATIVE

Sun Tzu said:

In war, the general receives his commands from the sovereign.

Having collected an army and concentrated his forces, he must blend and harmonize the different elements thereof before pitching his camp.

men's motivations

WEALTH

POWER

PRIDE

After that comes tactical maneuvering, than which there is nothing more difficult.

The difficulty of tactical maneuvering consists in turning the devious into the direct, and misfortune into gain.

Thus, to take a long and circuitous route, after enticing the enemy out of the way, and though starting after him, to contrive to reach the goal before him, shows knowledge of the artifice of deviation.

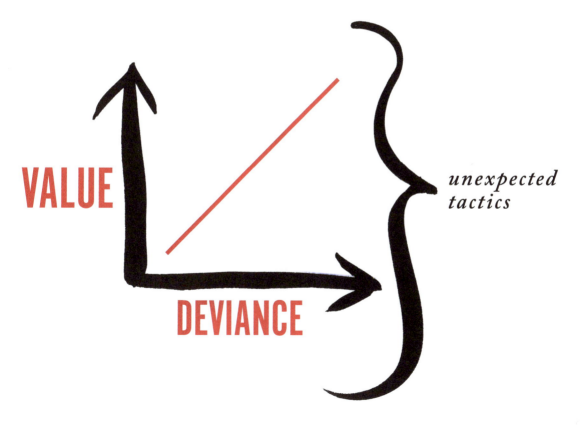

Maneuvering with an army is advantageous; with an undisciplined multitude, most dangerous.

doomed team

UNCOORDINATED

DISORGANIZED

UNDISCIPLINED

If you set a fully equipped army in march in order to snatch an advantage, the chances are that you will be too late.

On the other hand, to detach a flying column for the purpose involves the sacrifice of its baggage and stores.

Thus, if you order your men to roll up their buff-coats, and make forced marches without halting day or night, covering double the usual distance at a stretch, doing a hundred *li* in order to wrest an advantage, the leaders of all your three divisions will fall into the hands of the enemy.

AGILE

HEAVY BAGGAGE

USEFUL

TIRED

WELL RESTED

BURDENED

The stronger men will be in front, the jaded ones will fall behind, and on this plan only one-tenth of your army will reach its destination.

If you march fifty *li* in order to outmaneuver the enemy, you will lose the leader of your first division, and only half your force will reach the goal.

If you march thirty *li* with the same object, two-thirds of your army will arrive.

know what you are willing to spend

COSTS

CALCULATION

CONSERVATION

We may take it then that an army without its baggage-train is lost; without provisions, it is lost; without bases of supply, it is lost.

We cannot enter into alliances until we are acquainted with the designs of our neighbors.

We are not fit to lead an army on the march unless we are familiar with the face of the country—its mountains and forests, its pitfalls and precipices, its marshes and swamps.

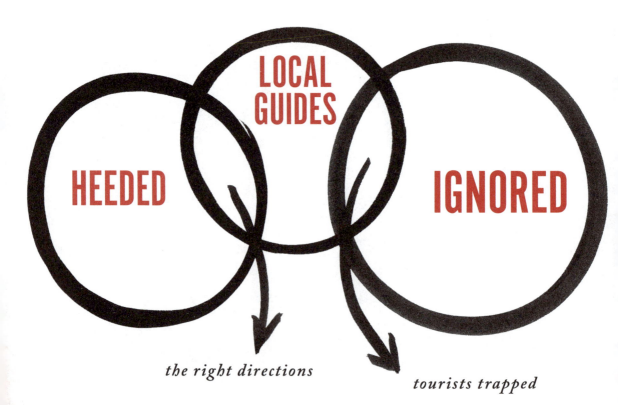

We shall be unable to turn natural advantage to account unless we make use of local guides.

HOME-FIELD ADVANTAGE

COMPETITIVE EDGE

NATURAL RESOURCES

In war, practice dissimulation, and you will succeed.

Move only if there is a real advantage to be gained.

Whether to concentrate or to divide your troops must
be decided by circumstances.

VICTORY

LOVE

WAR

PRETENSE

Let your rapidity be that of the wind, your compactness that of the forest.

In raiding and plundering be like fire, in immovability like a mountain.

Let your plans be dark and impenetrable as night, and when you move, fall like a thunderbolt.

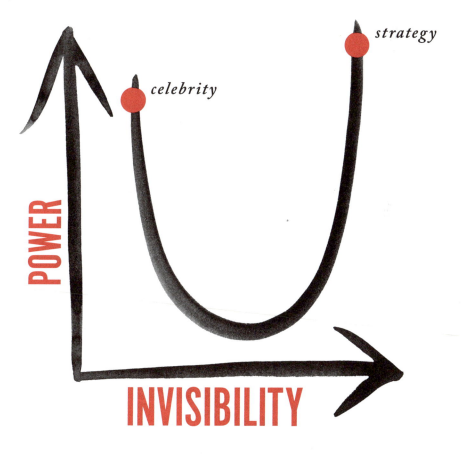

When you plunder a countryside, let the spoil be divided amongst your men; when you capture new territory, cut it up into allotments for the benefit of the soldiery.

RESPECT

GENEROSITY

loyalty

Ponder and deliberate before you make a move.

He will conquer who has learnt the artifice of deviation.

Such is the art of maneuvering.

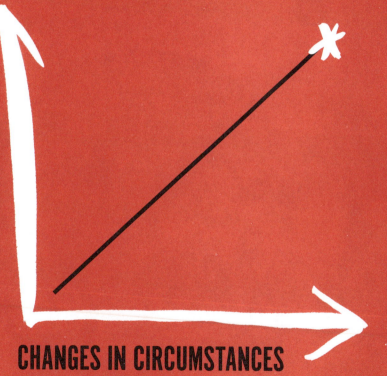

CHANGES
IN PLANS

CHANGES IN CIRCUMSTANCES

*brilliant maneuvers

> The Book of Army Management says:
>
> On the field of battle, the spoken word does not carry far enough: hence the institution of gongs and drums.
>
> Nor can ordinary objects be seen clearly enough: hence the institution of banners and flags.
>
> Gongs and drums, banners and flags, are means whereby the ears and eyes of the host may be focused on one particular point.

OBVIOUS

effective propaganda

UBIQUITOUS

The host thus forming a single united body, it is impossible either for the brave to advance alone, or for the cowardly to retreat alone.

This is the art of handling large masses of men.

ALIGNMENT

GOALS

ability to move forward

In night-fighting, then, make much use of signal-fires and drums, and in fighting by day, of flags and banners, as a means of influencing the ears and eyes of your army.

A whole army may be robbed of its spirit; a commander-in-chief may be robbed of his presence of mind.

Now a soldier's spirit is keenest in the morning; by noonday, it has begun to flag; and in the evening, his mind is bent only on returning to camp.

A clever general, therefore, avoids an army when its spirit is keen, but attacks it when it is sluggish and inclined to return.

This is the art of studying moods.

EXHAUSTED

disengaged

OVERWORKED

Disciplined and calm, to await the appearance of disorder and hubbub amongst the enemy: This is the art of retaining self-possession.

DISORDER RISES FAITH SINKS

death by internal combustion

To be near the goal while the enemy is still far from it, to wait at ease while the enemy is toiling and struggling, to be well-fed while the enemy is famished: This is the art of husbanding one's strength.

To refrain from intercepting an enemy whose banners are in perfect order, to refrain from attacking an army drawn up in calm and confident array: This is the art of studying circumstances.

timing the market

CUNNING

PATIENCE

It is a military axiom not to advance uphill against the enemy, nor to oppose him when he comes downhill.

Do not pursue an enemy who simulates flight; do not attack soldiers whose temper is keen.

Do not swallow bait offered by the enemy.

Do not interfere with an army that is returning home.

morale boosters

When you surround an army, leave an outlet free.

Do not press a desperate foe too hard.

Such is the art of warfare.

ROOM
TO MOVE

COMPOSURE

*flying first class &
winning negotiations*

CHAPTER 8
VARIATION IN TACTICS

VISUALIZE YOUR ALTERNATIVES

Sun Tzu said:

In war, the general receives his commands from the sovereign, collects his army, and concentrates his forces.

DEFEND

EARN

respect

AUTHORITY

 frustration

RESPONSIBILITY

When in difficult country, do not encamp.

In country where high roads intersect, join hands with your allies.

Do not linger in dangerously isolated positions.

In hemmed-in situations, you must resort to stratagem.

In a desperate position, you must fight.

DANGER

ISOLATION

never walk alone

There are roads which must not be followed, armies which must be not attacked, towns which must be besieged, positions which must not be contested, commands of the sovereign which must not be obeyed.

suggestions

WISDOM

laws

NAÏVETÉ

RULES

The general who thoroughly understands the advantages that accompany variation of tactics knows how to handle his troops.

The general who does not understand these, may be well acquainted with the configuration of the country, yet he will not be able to turn his knowledge to practical account.

only valuable when acted upon

STREET SMARTS

BOOK LEARNING

So, the student of war who is unversed in the art of war of varying his plans, even though he be acquainted with the Five Advantages, will fail to make the best use of his men.

Hence in the wise leader's plans, considerations of advantage and of disadvantage will be blended together.

situational

ACTUAL

SOLUTION

CONFLICT

THEORETICAL

wonky

If our expectation of advantage be tempered in this way, we may succeed in accomplishing the essential part of our schemes.

If, on the other hand, in the midst of difficulties we are always ready to seize an advantage, we may extricate ourselves from misfortune.

BOOKS WRITTEN ABOUT YOU

HUBRIS

Reduce the hostile chiefs by inflicting damage on them; and make trouble for them, and keep them constantly engaged; hold out specious allurements, and make them rush to any given point.

VICIOUS

RELENTLESS

ANNOYING

*mean girls &
telemarketers*

The art of war teaches us to rely not on the likelihood of the enemy's not coming, but on our own readiness to receive him; not on the chance of his not attacking, but rather on the fact that we have made our position unassailable.

TRUE

KNOWN

always less than you'd like

There are five dangerous faults which may affect a general:

1. Recklessness, which leads to destruction;

2. Cowardice, which leads to capture;

3. A hasty temper, which can be provoked by insults;

4. A delicacy of honor, which is sensitive to shame;

5. Over-solicitude for his men, which exposes him to worry and trouble.

These are the five besetting sins of a general, ruinous to the conduct of war.

IMPULSIVITY

EGO

MICROMANAGEMENT

Jerk

When an army is overthrown and its leader slain, the cause will surely be found amongst these five dangerous faults.

Let them be a subject of meditation.

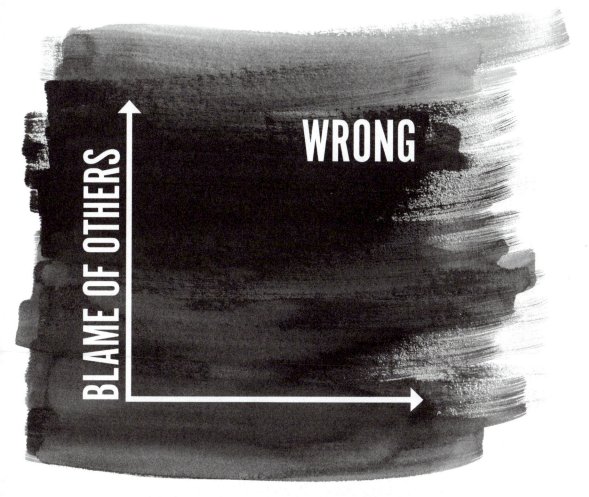

CHAPTER 9
THE ARMY ON THE MARCH

VISUALIZE YOUR SURROUNDINGS

Sun Tzu said:

We come now to the question of encamping the army, and observing signs of the enemy.

Pass quickly over mountains, and keep in the neighborhood of valleys.

Camp in high places, facing the sun. Do not climb heights in order to fight.

So much for mountain warfare.

DEFEAT

FIGHT

A

EMPLOY

VICTORY

A = the laws of physics & talented people

After crossing a river, you should get far away from it.

When an invading force crosses a river in its onward march, do not advance to meet it in mid-stream.

It will be best to let half the army get across, and then deliver your attack.

If you are anxious to fight, you should not go to meet the invader near a river which he has to cross.

Moor your craft higher up than the enemy, and facing the sun.

Do not move upstream to meet the enemy.

So much for river warfare.

LIFE LEFT IN YOU

salmon & people writing resignation letters

TIME SPENT SWIMMING UPSTREAM

In crossing salt-marshes, your sole concern should be to get over them quickly, without any delay.

If forced to fight in a salt-marsh, you should have water and grass near you, and get your back to a clump of trees.

So much for operations in salt-marches.

NO CLEAR PATHS OUT

FEELING STUCK

how to waste your life

WAITING FOR THINGS TO FIRM UP

In dry, level country, take up an easily accessible position with rising ground to your right and on your rear, so that the danger may be in front, and safety lie behind.

So much for campaigning in flat country.

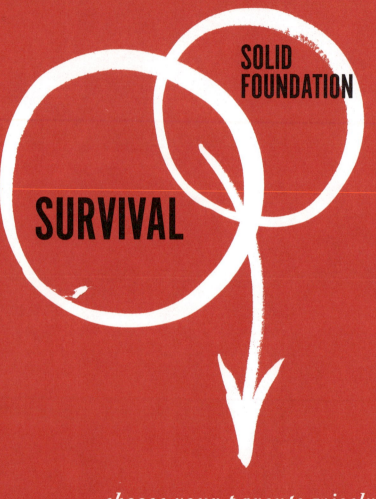

SOLID FOUNDATION

SURVIVAL

choose your parents wisely

These are the four useful branches of military knowledge which enabled the Yellow Emperor to vanquish four several sovereigns.

1. All armies prefer high ground to low and sunny places to dark.

If you are careful of your men, and camp on hard ground, the army will be free from disease of every kind, and this will spell victory.

destroys 99% of harmful pests

TRUTH

SUNLIGHT

2. When you come to a hill or a bank, occupy the sunny side, with the slope on your right rear.

Thus you will at once act for the benefit of your soldiers and utilize the natural advantages of the ground.

3. When, in consequence of heavy rains up-country, a river which you wish to ford is swollen and flecked with foam, you must wait until it subsides.

everything

CHANGES

TIME

4. Country in which there are precipitous cliffs with torrents running between, deep natural hollows, confined places, tangled thickets, quagmires, and crevasses should be left with all possible speed and not approached.

While we keep away from such places, we should get the enemy to approach them; while we face them, we should let the enemy have them on his rear.

FLED THE
SCENE

not all who
wander are lost

DID NOT
FEEL SAFE

If in the neighborhood of your camp there should be any hilly country, ponds surrounded by aquatic grass, hollow basins filled with reeds, or woods with thick undergrowth, they must be carefully routed out and searched; for these are places where men in ambush or insidious spies are likely to be lurking.

Sasquatch costumes

THICK WOODS

TREACHERY

moonshiners

PONDS SURROUNDED BY GRASS

HILLY COUNTRY

office parks

When the enemy is close at hand and remains quiet, he is relying on the natural strength of his position.

When he keeps aloof and tries to provoke a battle, he is anxious for the other side to advance.

If his place of encampment is easy of access, he is tendering a bait.

KINGS

ASSASSINS

beware: plot twist ahead

POWER

SILENCE

Movement amongst the trees of a forest shows that the enemy is advancing.

The appearance of a number of screens in the midst of thick grass means that the enemy wants to make us suspicious.

The rising of birds in their flight is the sign of an ambuscade.

Startled beasts indicate that a sudden attack is coming.

SAFETY

ENVIRONMENTAL CHANGES

seasons

THREAT

storms

When there is dust rising in a high column, it is the sign of chariots advancing; when the dust is low, but spread over a wide area, it betokens the approach of infantry.

When it branches out in different directions, it shows that parties have been sent to collect firewood.

A few clouds of dust moving to and fro signify that the army is encamping.

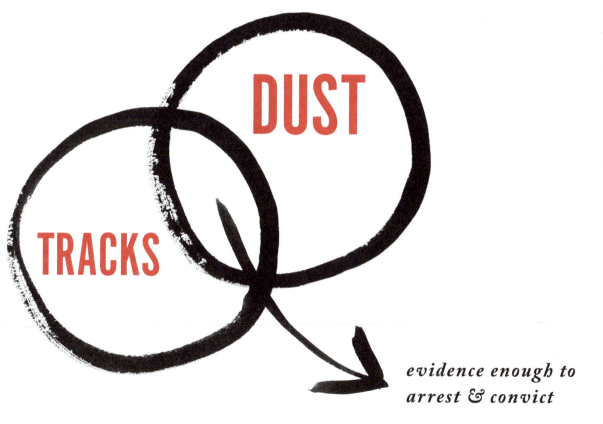

DUST

TRACKS

evidence enough to arrest & convict

Humble words and increased preparations are signs that the enemy is about to advance.

Violent language and driving forward as if to the attack are signs that he will retreat.

When the light chariots come out first and take up a position on the wings, it is a sign that the enemy is forming for battle.

Peace proposals unaccompanied by a sworn covenant indicate a plot.

When there is much running about and the soldiers fall into rank, it means that the critical moment has come.

When some are seen advancing and some retreating, it is a lure.

SNEAKING AROUND

CRITICAL MOMENT

busted

When the soldiers stand leaning on their spears, they are faint from want of food.

If those who are sent to draw water begin by drinking themselves, the army is suffering from thirst.

If the enemy sees an advantage to be gained and makes no effort to secure it, the soldiers are exhausted.

If birds gather on any spot, it is unoccupied.

Clamor by night betokens nervousness.

HOW GOOD A MUTINY SOUNDS

CASES OF SCURVY ONBOARD

If there is disturbance in the camp, the general's authority is weak.

If the banners and flags are shifted about, sedition is afoot.

If the officers are angry, it means that the men are weary.

*tired toddlers & offices
with high turnover*

AGITATION

TANTRUMS

ANXIETY

When an army feeds its horses with grain and kills its cattle for food, and when the men do not hang their cooking-pots over the camp-fires, showing that they will not return to their tents, you may know that they are determined to fight to the death.

The sight of men whispering together in small knots or speaking in subdued tones points to disaffection amongst the rank and file.

off to war or to the altar

COLD FEET

SWEATY PALMS

NERVOUSNESS

DEPTH OF COMMITMENT

Too frequent rewards signify that the enemy is at the end of his resources; too many punishments betray a condition of dire distress.

DESPERATE MEASURES

DESPERATE TIMES

beating & bribing

To begin by bluster, but afterwards to take fright at the enemy's numbers, shows a supreme lack of intelligence.

UNDERDELIVER

OVERPROMISE

how to lose deals & enrage people

When envoys are sent with compliments in their mouths, it is a sign that the enemy wishes for a truce.

If the enemy's troops march up angrily and remain facing ours for a long time without either joining battle or taking themselves off again, the situation is one that demands great vigilance and circumspection.

how fights start & relationships end

CRUEL WORDS

SNEERS

POSTURING

If our troops are no more in number than the enemy, that is amply sufficient; it only means that no direct attack can be made.

What we can do is simply to concentrate all our available strength, keep a close watch on the enemy, and obtain reinforcements.

the path to victory is revealed

WATCHFULNESS

PATIENCE

He who exercises no forethought but makes light of his opponents is sure to be captured by them.

WHO YOU MOCK

WHO YOU IGNORE

who you should fear

If soldiers are punished before they have grown attached to you, they will not prove submissive; and, unless submissive, then will be practically useless.

If, when the soldiers have become attached to you, punishments are not enforced, they will still be useless.

Therefore soldiers must be treated in the first instance with humanity, but kept under control by means of iron discipline.

This is a certain road to victory.

FEAR

ATTACHMENT

abusive relationships

If in training soldiers, commands are habitually enforced, the army will be well disciplined; if not, its discipline will be bad.

If a general shows confidence in his men but always insists on his orders being obeyed, the gain will be mutual.

CHAPTER 10
TERRAIN

VISUALIZE
YOUR
GAME PLAN

Sun Tzu said:

We may distinguish six kinds of terrain, to wit:

1. Accessible ground;

2. Entangling ground;

3. Temporizing ground;

4. Narrow passes;

5. Precipitous heights;

6. Positions at a great distance from the enemy.

LESSONS LEARNED

PLACES VISITED

get out there

Ground which can be freely traversed by both sides is called accessible.

With regard to ground of this nature, be before the enemy in occupying the raised and sunny spots, and carefully guard your line of supplies.

Then you will be able to fight with advantage.

call shotgun & dominate your market

Ground which can be abandoned but is hard to re-occupy is called entangling.

From a position of this sort, if the enemy is unprepared, you may sally forth and defeat him.

But if the enemy is prepared for your coming, and you fail to defeat him, then, return being impossible, disaster will ensue.

PROPERTY DISPUTES

REDEFINED MAPS

INVADING SETTLERS

gentrifying neighborhoods & the Middle East

When the position is such that neither side will gain by making the first move, it is called temporizing ground.

In a position of this sort, even though the enemy should offer us an attractive bait, it will be advisable not to stir forth, but rather to retreat, thus enticing the enemy in his turn; then, when part of his army has come out, we may deliver our attack with advantage.

gridlock ←

4-WAY STOP

EXCESSIVE POLITENESS

With regard to narrow passes, if you can occupy them first, let them be strongly garrisoned and await the advent of the enemy.

Should the army forestall you in occupying a pass, do not go after him if the pass is fully garrisoned, but only if it is weakly garrisoned.

BRIDGES

TUNNELS

MASSIVE TOOLS

With regard to precipitous heights, if you are beforehand with your adversary, you should occupy the raised and sunny spots, and there wait for him to come up.

If the enemy has occupied them before you, do not follow him, but retreat and try to entice him away.

> If you are situated at a great distance from the enemy, and the strength of the two armies is equal, it is not easy to provoke a battle, and fighting will be to your disadvantage.

BUILT FOR DESTRUCTION

SO MANY ARMS

nukes & Kali

These six are the principles connected with Earth.

The general who has attained a responsible post must be careful to study them.

keeping your foot out of your mouth

MINEFIELDS AVOIDED

AWARENESS OF ISSUES

1. Now an army is exposed to six several calamities, not arising from natural causes, but from faults for which the general is responsible.

These are:

i. Flight;

ii. Insubordination;

iii. Collapse;

iv. Ruin;

v. Disorganization;

vi. Rout.

DISORDER

the fall of civilization

DESPAIR

2. Other conditions being equal, if one force is hurled against another ten times its size, the result will be the flight of the former.

bullets & insults

3. When the common soldiers are too strong and their officers too weak, the result is insubordination.

When the officers are too strong and the common soldiers too weak, the result is collapse.

functionality

STRONG
LEADERSHIP

COMPLIANT
UNDERLINGS

A CLUE OR TWO

4. When the higher officers are angry and insubordinate, and on meeting the enemy give battle on their own account from a feeling of resentment, before the commander-in-chief can tell whether or not he is in a position to fight, the result is ruin.

SUBJUGATION

INSUBORDINATION

A = respect is demanded

5. When the general is weak and without authority; when his orders are not clear and distinct; when there are no fixed duties assigned to officers and men, and the ranks are formed in a slovenly haphazard manner, the result is utter disorganization.

FLAKY

DANGEROUS

blizzards &
weak bosses

6. When a general, unable to estimate the enemy's strength, allows an inferior force to engage a larger one, or hurls a weak detachment against a powerful one, and neglects to place picked soldiers in the front rank, the result must be a rout.

CHANCES YOU WILL DIE ALONE

NEGLECT OF DEPENDENTS

These six ways of courting defeat must be carefully noted by the general who has attained a responsible post.

BACKBONE

BACKUP

good work gets done

The natural formation of the country is the soldier's best ally; but a power of estimating the adversary, of controlling the forces of victory, and of shrewdly calculating difficulties, dangers, and distances, constitutes the test of a great general.

He who knows these things, and in fighting puts his knowledge into practice, will win his battles.

He who knows them not, nor practices them, will surely be defeated.

LOGISTICS

SOCIOLOGY

GEOGRAPHY

navigating new lands

If fighting is sure to result in victory, then you must fight, even though the ruler forbid it; if fighting will not result in victory, then you must not fight even at the ruler's bidding.

The general who advances without coveting fame and retreats without fearing disgrace, whose only thought is to protect his country and do good service for his sovereign, is the jewel of the kingdom.

FACTS > EMOTIONS

NATION > SELF

REAL > RUMOR

the logic of leadership

Regard your soldiers as your children, and they will follow you into the deepest valleys; look upon them as your own beloved sons, and they will stand by you even unto death.

If, however, you are indulgent, but unable to make your authority felt; kind-hearted, but unable to enforce your commands; and incapable, moreover, of quelling disorder: Then your soldiers must be likened to spoilt children; they are useless for any practical purpose.

SINS ENCOURAGED

INDULGENCES GIVEN

If we know that our own men are in a condition to attack, but are unaware that the enemy is not open to attack, we have gone only halfway towards victory.

If we know that the enemy is open to attack, but are unaware that our own men are not in a condition to attack, we have gone only halfway towards victory.

If we know that the enemy is open to attack, and also know that our men are in a condition to attack, but are unaware that the nature of the ground makes fighting impracticable, we have still gone only halfway towards victory.

BLIND SPOTS

BURNING

ACCIDENTS

actual car crashes & metaphorical train wrecks

Hence the experienced soldier, once in motion, is never bewildered; once he has broken camp, he is never at a loss.

Hence the saying: If you know the enemy and know yourself, your victory will not stand in doubt; if you know Heaven and know Earth, you may make your victory complete.

FREQUENCY OF FLUSTER

EXPERIENCE

CHAPTER 11

THE NINE SITUATIONS

VISUALIZE YOUR OUTCOMES

Sun Tzu said:

The art of war recognizes nine varieties of ground:

1. Dispersive ground;

2. Facile ground;

3. Contentious ground;

4. Open ground;

5. Ground of intersecting highways;

6. Serious ground;

7. Difficult ground;

8. Hemmed-in ground;

9. Desperate ground.

EXPLORING

vacation

LEAVING HOME

CONQUERING

work

When a chieftain is fighting in his own territory, it is dispersive ground.

When he has penetrated into hostile territory, but to no great distance, it is facile ground.

Ground the possession of which imports great advantage to either side, is contentious ground.

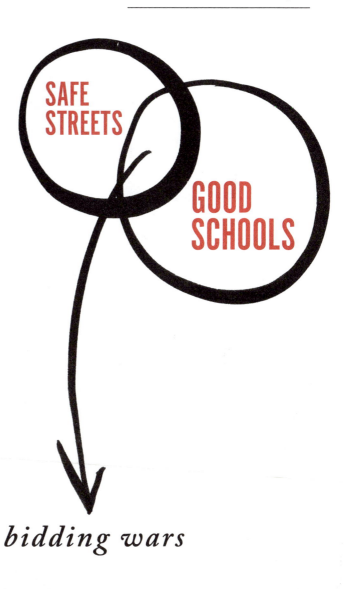

SAFE STREETS

GOOD SCHOOLS

bidding wars

Ground on which each side has liberty of movement is open ground.

Ground which forms the key to three contiguous states, so that he who occupies it first has most of the Empire at his command, is a ground of intersecting highways.

TRADE

DIPLOMACY

defend the ports

When an army has penetrated into the heart of a hostile country, leaving a number of fortified cities in its rear, it is serious ground.

Mountain forests, rugged steeps, marshes, and fens—all country that is hard to traverse: This is difficult ground.

reaching great heights

SLOW GOING

TREACHEROUS

WORTH IT

Ground which is reached through narrow gorges, and from which we can only retire by tortuous paths, so that a small number of the enemy would suffice to crush a large body of our men: This is hemmed-in ground.

Ground on which we can only be saved from destruction by fighting without delay, is desperate ground.

freedom from desperation

DIGNITY

OPTIONS

On dispersive ground, therefore, fight not.

On facile ground, halt not.

On contentious ground, attack not.

On open ground, do not try to block the enemy's way.

On the ground of intersecting highways, join hands with your allies.

On serious ground, gather in plunder.

In difficult ground, keep steadily on the march.

On hemmed-in ground, resort to stratagem.

On desperate ground, fight.

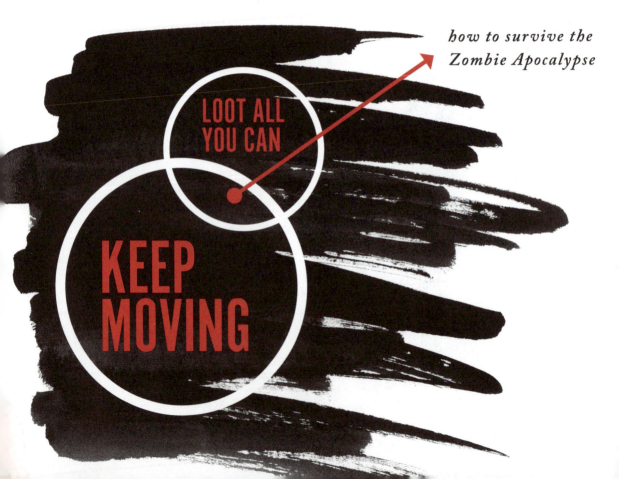

how to survive the Zombie Apocalypse

LOOT ALL YOU CAN

KEEP MOVING

Those who were called skillful leaders of old knew how to drive a wedge between the enemy's front and rear; to prevent cooperation between his large and small divisions; to hinder the good troops from rescuing the bad, the officers from rallying their men.

*what holds
a team together*

COMMUNICATION

CAMARADERIE

When the enemy's men were united, they managed to keep them in disorder.

When it was to their advantage, they made a forward move; when otherwise, they stopped still.

capitalize *strategize*

CHASE PREY WATCH

HOW TO THIN A HERD

If asked how to cope with a great host of the enemy in orderly array and on the point of marching to the attack, I should say:

"Begin by seizing something which your opponent holds dear; then he will be amenable to your will."

LIVELIHOOD

PRIDE

LOVED ONES

fulcrums of manipulation

Rapidity is the essence of war:

Take advantage of the enemy's unreadiness, make your way by unexpected routes, and attack unguarded spots.

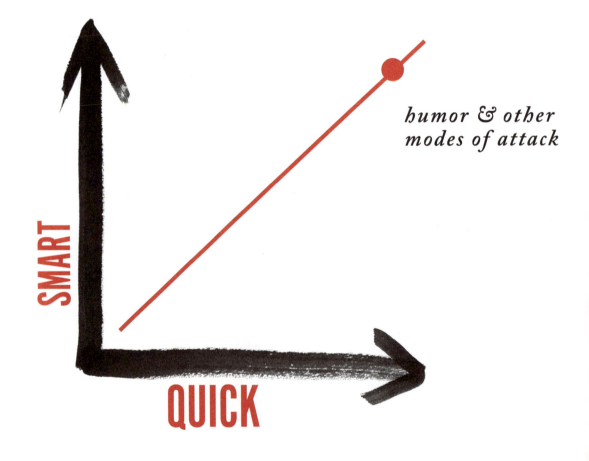

humor & other modes of attack

The following are the principles to be observed by an invading force:

The further you penetrate into a country, the greater will be the solidarity of your troops, and thus the defenders will not prevail against you.

Make forays in fertile country in order to supply your army with food.

PERCEPTION

MOMENTUM

If you're thinking you're winning or losing, you're correct.

Carefully study the well-being of your men, and do not overtax them.

Concentrate your energy and hoard your strength.

Keep your army continually on the move, and devise unfathomable plans.

apathy

ROT

MACHINERY
& MARRIAGES

RUN

*regular
maintenance*

Throw your soldiers into positions whence there is no escape, and they will prefer death to flight. If they will face death, there is nothing they may not achieve.

Officers and men alike will put forth their uttermost strength.

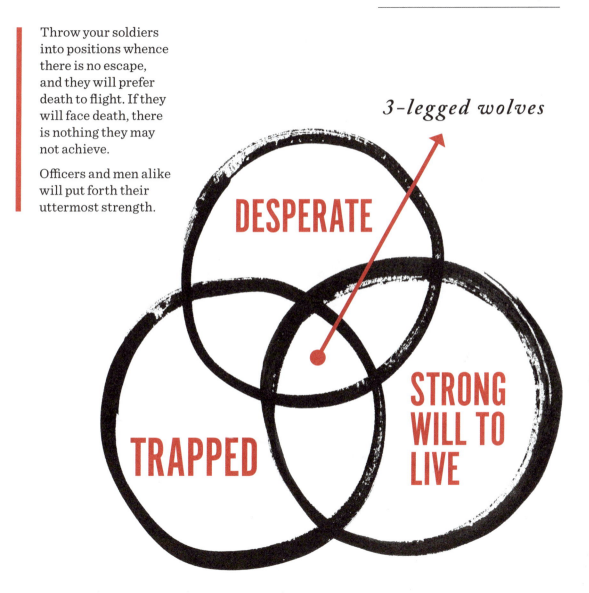

3-legged wolves

DESPERATE

TRAPPED

STRONG WILL TO LIVE

Soldiers when in desperate straits lose the sense of fear.

If there is no place of refuge, they will stand firm.

If they are in hostile country, they will show a stubborn front.

If there is no help for it, they will fight hard.

Thus, without waiting to be marshaled, the soldiers will be constantly on the qui vive; without waiting to be asked, they will do your will; without restrictions, they will be faithful; without giving orders, they can be trusted.

Prohibit the taking of omens, and do away with superstitious doubts.

Then, until death itself comes, no calamity need be feared.

If our soldiers are not overburdened with money, it is not because they have a distaste for riches; if their lives are not unduly long, it is not because they are disinclined to longevity.

WEALTHY

HEALTHY

WISE

no thanks to superstitions

On the day they are ordered out to battle, your soldiers may weep, those sitting up bedewing their garments, and those lying down letting the tears run down their cheeks.

But let them once be brought to bay, and they will display the courage of a Chu or a Kuei.

The skillful tactician may be likened to the shuai-jan.

Now the shuai-jan is a snake that is found in the Ch'ang mountains.

Strike at its head, and you will be attacked by its tail; strike at its tail, and you will be attacked by its head; strike at its middle, and you will be attacked by head and tail both.

Asked if an army can be made to imitate the shuai-jan, I should answer, Yes.

For the men of Wu and the men of Yueh are enemies; yet if they are crossing a river in the same boat and are caught by a storm, they will come to each other's assistance just as the left hand helps the right.

not to be trifled with

RESILIENT

PREPARED

FLEXIBLE

Hence it is not enough to put one's trust in the tethering of horses, and the burying of chariot wheels in the ground.

The principle on which to manage an army is to set up one standard of courage which all must reach.

How to make the best of both strong and weak—that is a question involving the proper use of ground.

Thus the skillful general conducts his army just as though he were leading a single man, willy-nilly, by the hand.

It is the business of a general to be quiet and thus ensure secrecy; upright and just, and thus maintain order.

He must be able to mystify his officers and men by false reports and appearances, and thus keep them in total ignorance.

By altering his arrangements and changing his plans, he keeps the enemy without definite knowledge.

By shifting his camp and taking circuitous routes, he prevents the enemy from anticipating his purpose.

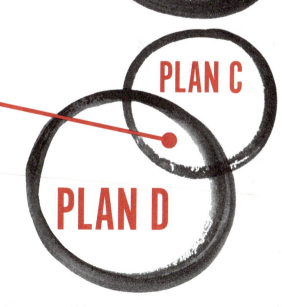

At the critical moment, the leader of an army acts like one who has climbed up a height and then kicks away the ladder behind him.

He carries his men deep into hostile territory before he shows his hand.

He burns his boats and breaks his cooking-pots; like a shepherd driving a flock of sheep, he drives his men this way and that, and nothing knows whither he is going.

To muster his host and bring it into danger: This may be termed the business of the general.

innovate or die

DANGER

ROUTINE

DEFEATABLE

PREDICTABLE

The different measures suited to the nine varieties of ground; the expediency of aggressive or defensive tactics; and the fundamental laws of human nature: These are things that must most certainly be studied.

WHERE

WHO

WHEN

vital information

When invading hostile territory, the general principle is, that penetrating deeply brings cohesion; penetrating but a short way means dispersion.

HEDGE

WAFFLE

fail

When you leave your own country behind, and take your army across neighborhood territory, you find yourself on critical ground.

When there are means of communication on all four sides, the ground is one of intersecting highways.

When you penetrate deeply into a country, it is serious ground.

When you penetrate but a little way, it is facile ground.

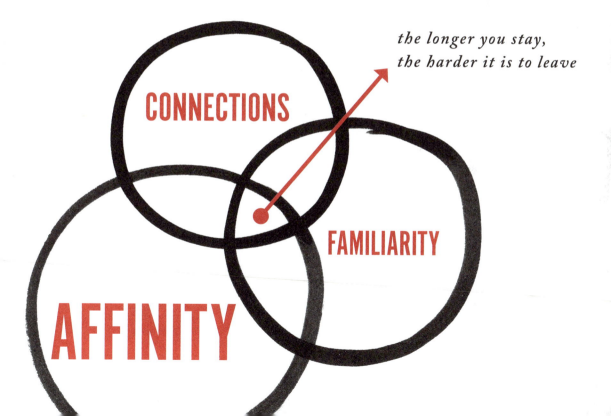

the longer you stay, the harder it is to leave

When you have the enemy's strongholds on your rear, and narrow passes in front, it is hemmed-in ground.

When there is no place of refuge at all, it is desperate ground.

Therefore, on dispersive ground, I would inspire my men with unity of purpose.

On facile ground, I would see that there is close connection between all parts of my army.

On contentious ground, I would hurry up my rear.

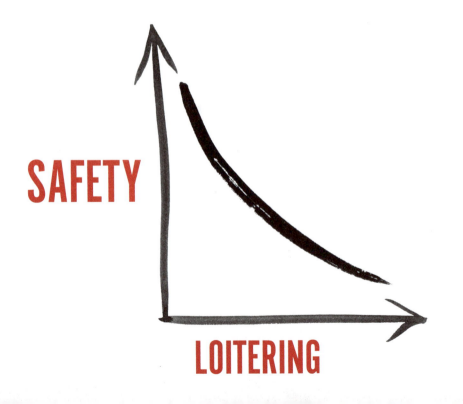

SAFETY

LOITERING

On open ground, I would keep a vigilant eye on my defenses.

On ground of intersecting highways, I would consolidate my alliances.

On serious ground, I would try to ensure a continuous stream of supplies.

On difficult ground, I would keep pushing on along the road.

STRESS

TRAVEL

a well-packed bag & a full tank of gas

On hemmed-in ground, I would block any way of retreat.

On desperate ground, I would proclaim to my soldiers the hopelessness of saving their lives.

For it is the soldier's disposition to offer an obstinate resistance when surrounded, to fight hard when he cannot help himself, and to obey promptly when he has fallen into danger.

VIABLE EXIT STRATEGIES

less than full commitment

PERMISSION TO LEAVE

We cannot enter into alliance with neighboring princes until we are acquainted with their designs.

We are not fit to lead an army on the march unless we are familiar with the face of the country—its mountains and forests, its pitfalls and precipices, its marshes and swamps.

We shall be unable to turn natural advantages to account unless we make use of local guides.

CONTEMPTIBLE

carpetbaggers
& invasive
species

NEW TO THE AREA & LOOKING TO TAKE OVER

To be ignored of any one of the following four or five principles does not befit a warlike prince.

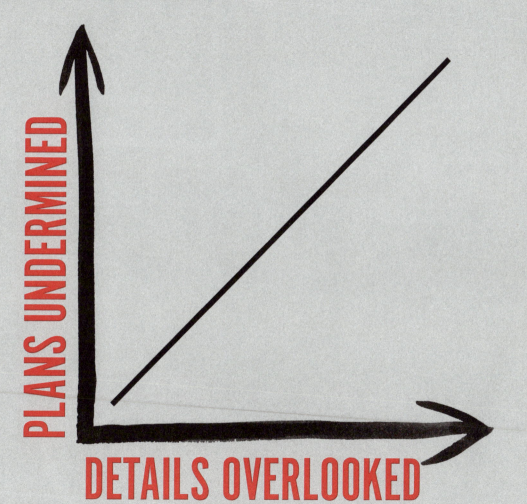

When a warlike prince attacks a powerful state, his generalship shows itself in preventing the concentration of the enemy's forces.

He overawes his opponents, and their allies are prevented from joining against him.

Hence he does not strive to ally himself with all and sundry, nor does he foster the power of other states.

He carries out his own secret designs, keeping his antagonists in awe.

Thus he is able to capture their cities and overthrow their kingdoms.

INTIMIDATION

COMPOSURE

STATURE

SWOON

REPUTATION

Bestow rewards without regard to rule, issue orders without regard to previous arrangements; and you will be able to handle a whole army as though you had to do with but a single man.

MERITOCRACY

REWARDS

the American dream

Confront your soldiers with the deed itself; never let them know your design.

When the outlook is bright, bring it before their eyes; but tell them nothing when the situation is gloomy.

STRATEGY

PLANS

career

TACTICS

work

Place your army in deadly peril, and it will survive; plunge it into desperate straits, and it will come off in safety.

For it is precisely when a force has fallen into harm's way that it is capable of striking a blow for victory.

Success in warfare is gained by carefully accommodating ourselves to the enemy's purpose.

By persistently hanging on the enemy's flank, we shall succeed in the long run in killing the commander-in-chief.

This is called ability to accomplish a thing by sheer cunning.

MANIPULATION

INFORMATION

On the day that you take up your command, block the frontier passes, destroy the official tallies, and stop the passage of all emissaries.

Be stern in the council-chamber, so that you may control the situation.

If the enemy leaves a door open, you must rush in.

PERCEIVED POWER

ASSERTIVENESS

PERCEIVED WEAKNESS

HESITATION

Forestall your opponent by seizing what he holds dear, and subtly contrive to time his arrival on the ground.

CONTAIN THEM

KEEP THEM BUSY

SEPARATE THEM

schools & prisons

Walk in the path defined by rule, and accommodate yourself to the enemy until you can fight a decisive battle.

At first, then, exhibit the coyness of a maiden, until the enemy gives you an opening; afterwards emulate the rapidity of a running hare, and it will be too late for the enemy to oppose you.

before your breakout move

LEARN THE RULES

PLAY NICELY

CHAPTER 12
THE ATTACK BY FIRE

VISUALIZE YOUR FLASHPOINTS

Sun Tzu said:

There are five ways of attacking with fire.

The first is to burn soldiers in their camp; the second is to burn stores; the third is to burn baggage trains; the fourth is to burn arsenals and magazines; the fifth is to hurl dropping fire amongst the enemy.

fire alarms in every home

SECURITY

SAFETY

In order to carry out an attack, we must have means available.

The material for raising fire should always be kept in readiness.

There is a proper season for making attacks with fire, and special days for starting a conflagration.

The proper season is when the weather is very dry; the special days are those when the moon is in the constellations of the Sieve, the Wall, the Wing or the Cross-bar; for these four are all days of rising wind.

CAPABILITY

OPPORTUNITY

right place, right time

In attacking with fire, one should be prepared to meet five possible developments:

1. When fire breaks out inside to enemy's camp, respond at once with an attack from without.

2. If there is an outbreak of fire, but the enemy's soldiers remain quiet, bide your time and do not attack.

3. When the force of the flames has reached its height, follow it up with an attack, if that is practicable; if not, stay where you are.

4. If it is possible to make an assault with fire from without, do not wait for it to break out within, but deliver your attack at a favorable moment.

5. When you start a fire, be to windward of it. Do not attack from the leeward.

A wind that rises in the daytime lasts long, but a night breeze soon falls.

HOLIDAY WEEKEND

when bad news is shared publicly

FRIDAY NIGHT

In every army, the five developments connected with fire must be known, the movements of the stars calculated, and a watch kept for the proper days.

Hence those who use fire as an aid to the attack show intelligence; those who use water as an aid to the attack gain an accession of strength.

FIRE

WATER

MEASUREMENT

cooking & tax assessment

By means of water, an enemy may be intercepted, but not robbed of all his belongings.

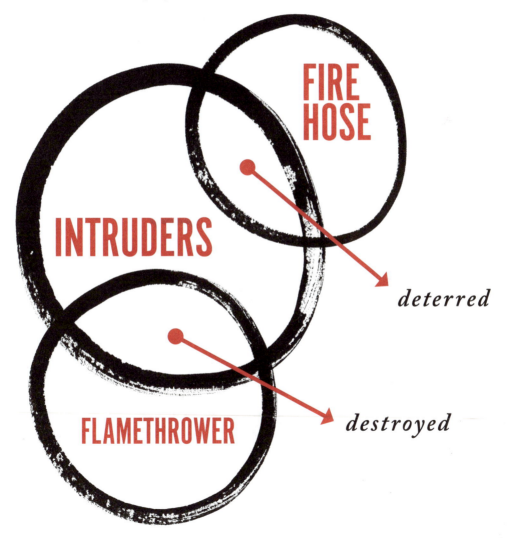

FIRE HOSE

INTRUDERS

deterred

FLAMETHROWER

destroyed

Unhappy is the fate of one who tries to win his battles and succeed in his attacks without cultivating the spirit of enterprise; for the result is waste of time and general stagnation.

Hence the saying:

The enlightened ruler lays his plans well ahead; the good general cultivates his resources.

INNOVATION

PLANS

CREATIVITY

what investors seek

Move not unless you see an advantage; use not your troops unless there is something to be gained; fight not unless the position is critical.

URGENCY

IMPORTANCE

speed up or slam on the brakes

No ruler should put troops into the field merely to gratify his own spleen; no general should fight a battle simply out of pique.

If it is to your advantage, make a forward move; if not, stay where you are.

IMPULSE

EGO

a danger to yourself and others

Anger may in time change to gladness; vexation may be succeeded by content.

But a kingdom that has once been destroyed can never come again into being; nor can the dead ever be brought back to life.

Hence the enlightened ruler is heedful, and the good general full of caution.

This is the way to keep a country at peace and an army intact.

CHAPTER 13
THE USE OF SPIES

VISUALIZE
YOUR
TRUTHS

Sun Tzu said:

Raising a host of a hundred thousand men and marching them great distances entails heavy loss on the people and a drain on the resources of the State.

The daily expenditure will amount to a thousand ounces of silver.

There will be commotion at home and abroad, and men will drop down exhausted on the highways.

As many as seven hundred thousand families will be impeded in their labor.

diplomacy is always cheaper

DOMESTIC COSTS

FOREIGN WARS

Hostile armies may face each other for years, striving for the victory which is decided in a single day.

This being so, to remain in ignorance of the enemy's condition simply because one grudges the outlay of a hundred ounces of silver in honors and emoluments, is the height of inhumanity.

One who acts thus is no leader of men, no present help to his sovereign, no master of victory.

A = grudges
B = resentments
C = jealousy
D = damage to self-interests

Thus, what enables the wise sovereign and the good general to strike and conquer, and achieve things beyond the reach of ordinary men, is foreknowledge.

Now this foreknowledge cannot be elicited from spirits; it cannot be obtained inductively from experience, nor by any deductive calculation.

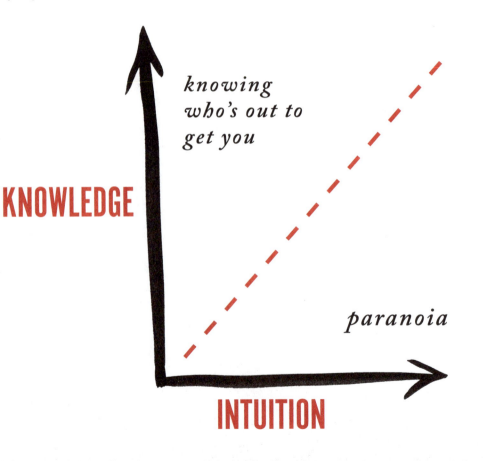

Knowledge of the enemy's dispositions can only be obtained from other men.

CONSPIRE
TO MEET

LISTEN
CLOSELY

GAIN
ADVANTAGES

courtship & espionage

Hence the use of spies, of whom there are five classes:

1. Local spies;

2. Inward spies;

3. Converted spies;

4. Doomed spies;

5. Surviving spies.

RARE EXPERTISE

HIGH DEMAND

rich spies

When these five kinds of spy are all at work, none can discover the secret system.

This is called "divine manipulation of the threads."

It is the sovereign's most precious faculty.

FIND ANOTHER SOURCE

journalism & philosophy

UNCOVER MORE TRUTH

Having local spies means employing the services of the inhabitants of a district.

Having inward spies, making use of officials of the enemy.

Having converted spies, getting hold of the enemy's spies and using them for our own purposes.

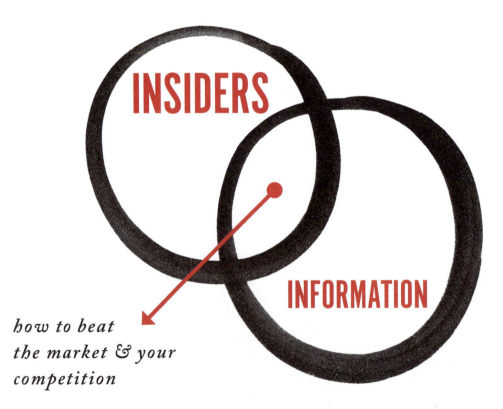

INSIDERS

INFORMATION

how to beat the market & your competition

Having doomed spies, doing certain things openly for purposes of deception, and allowing our spies to know of them and report them to the enemy.

Surviving spies, finally, are those who bring back news from the enemy's camp.

ENEMIES TO THWART

NOTHING TO LOSE

the double cross

Hence it is that which none in the whole army are more intimate relations to be maintained than with spies.

None should be more liberally rewarded.

In no other business should greater secrecy be preserved.

COST TO INSURE

VALUE OF ASSET

useful spies & other national treasures

Spies cannot be usefully employed without a certain intuitive sagacity.

They cannot be properly managed without benevolence and straightforwardness.

Without subtle ingenuity of mind, one cannot make certain of the truth of their reports.

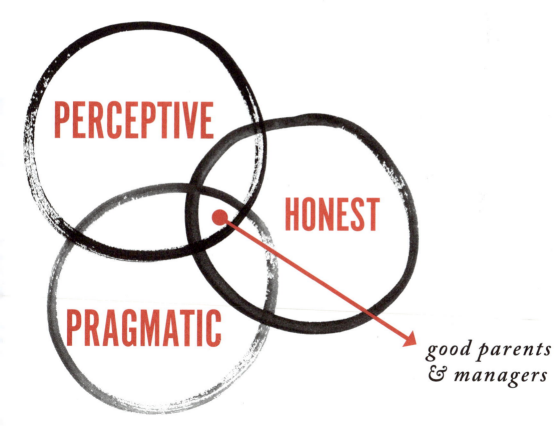

PERCEPTIVE

HONEST

PRAGMATIC

good parents & managers

Be subtle! be subtle!

and use your spies for every kind of business.

If a secret piece of news is divulged by a spy before the time is ripe, he must be put to death together with the man to whom the secret was told.

ALLIES

ABILITY TO KEEP A SECRET

Whether the object be to crush an army, to storm a city, or to assassinate an individual, it is always necessary to begin by finding out the names of the attendants, the aides-de-camp, and door-keepers and sentries of the general in command.

Our spies must be commissioned to ascertain these.

TROUBLE

STONES
LEFT
UNTURNED

*worms &
missed
opportunities*

The enemy's spies who have come to spy on us must be sought out, tempted with bribes, led away, and comfortably housed.

Thus they will become converted spies and available for our service.

WINE

DINE

LOBBY

how laws & babies are made

It is through the information brought by the converted spy that we are able to acquire and employ local and inward spies.

It is owing to his information, again, that we can cause the doomed spy to carry false tidings to the enemy.

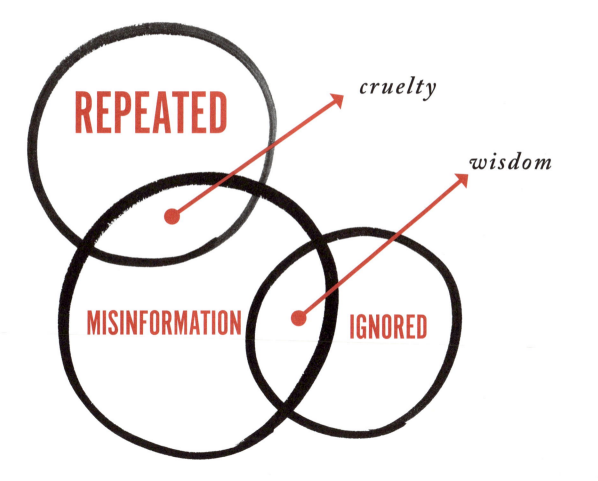

Lastly, it is by his information that the surviving spy can be used on appointed occasions.

The end and aim of spying in all its five varieties is knowledge of the enemy; and this knowledge can only be derived, in the first instance, from the converted spy.

Hence it is essential that the converted spy be treated with the utmost liberality.

Of old, the rise of the Yin dynasty was due to I Chih who had served under the Hsia.

Likewise, the rise of the Chou dynasty was due to Lu Ya who had served under the Yin.

oxymoronic danger

LOYALTY

SPIES

Hence it is only the enlightened ruler and the wise general who will use the highest intelligence of the army for purposes of spying and thereby they achieve great results.

Spies are a most important element in water, because on them depends an army's ability to move.

SUCCESS

in times of war & peace

APPLIED INTELLIGENCE

THE END